OUR PLANET OUR FUTURE

DEFENDING THE ANIMALS

Written by
Azra Limbada

Cavendish Square
New York

Published in 2022 by Cavendish Square Publishing, LLC
29 East 21st Street
New York, NY 10010

© 2020 Booklife Publishing
This edition is published by arrangement with Booklife Publishing

Website: cavendishsq.com

This publication represents the opinions and views of the author based on his or her
personal experience, knowledge, and research. The information in this book serves as
a general guide only. The author and publisher have used their best efforts in preparing
this book and disclaim liability rising directly or indirectly from the use and application of
this book.

All websites were available and accurate when this book was sent to press.

Edited by: John Wood
Designed by: Drue Rintoul

Cataloging-in-Publication Data
Names: Limbada, Azra.
Title: Defending the animals / Azra Limbada.
Description: New York : Cavendish Square, 2022. | Series: Our planet, our future |
Includes glossary and index.
Identifiers: ISBN 9781502663498 (pbk.) | ISBN 9781502663511 (library bound) |
ISBN 9781502663504 (6 pack) | ISBN 9781502663528 (ebook)
Subjects: LCSH: Wildlife conservation--Juvenile literature. | Environmental responsibility--
Juvenile literature.
Classification: LCC QL83.L563 2022 | DDC 333.95'4--dc23

Some of the images in this book illustrate individuals who are models. The depictions do
not imply actual situations or events.

CPSIA compliance information: Batch #CW22CSQ: For further information contact Cavendish Square Publishing LLC, New York, New York,
at 1-877-980-4450.

Printed in the United States of America

Find us on

PHOTO CREDITS

Images are courtesy of Shutterstock.com. With thanks to Getty Images, Thinkstock Photo and iStockphoto. Cover - Tristan Tan, John Wollwerth. 4&5 - Vladi333, vovan. 6&7 - Ondrej Prosicky, Batkova Elena.
8&9 - mr_renderman, Lycia W. 10&11 - Sergey Uryadnikov, Jay Ondreicka. 12&13 - metha1819, wavebreakmedia. 14&15 - Daniel Prudek, Brocreative. 16&17 - Don Mammoser, Hurst Photo. 18&19 - Alex East, Monkey
Business Images. 20&21 - lev radin, worapot noicharoen. 22&23 - Peter Radosa, eNjoy iStyle, Vitaly Zorkin, Hurst Photo, ANCH, xpixel.

CONTENTS

Words that look like this can be found in the glossary on page 24.

EARTH

Planet Earth is home to us all. There are so many beautiful places to see, from snowy mountains to the deep blue sea. Every corner of our world is full of life.

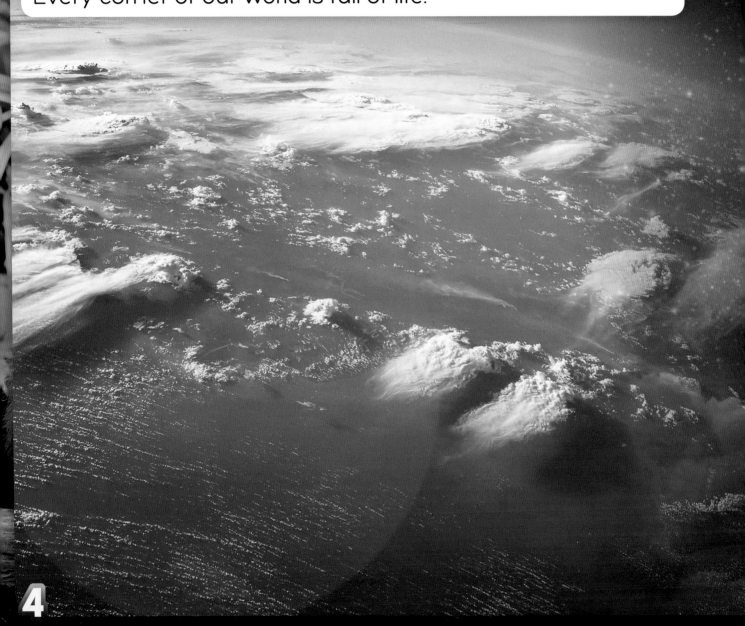

WHAT CAN YOU SEE?

Can you see the fluffy, white clouds?
Can you see the bright, shining stars?

EARTH IS THE PERFECT HOME FOR ALL LIVING THINGS.

ANIMALS

We share our planet with lots of different animals. There are millions of different <u>species</u> of animals on Earth!

DID YOU KNOW THAT HUMANS ARE A TYPE OF ANIMAL TOO?

It is our job to keep the planet safe. We need to work together to protect the <u>environment</u> and all the animals that share our home.

7

THE ECOSYSTEM

Animals and plants that live together in one area are all connected. This is called an ecosystem. Weather, <u>landscape,</u> and rocks are all part of an ecosystem.

THIS LAKE IS AN ECOSYSTEM.

IN AN ECOSYSTEM, EVERY ANIMAL OR PLANT HAS THEIR OWN PART TO PLAY.

Many ecosystems have been damaged or destroyed by humans. Humans cause lots of <u>pollution</u>, which is very harmful for many ecosystems.

THROWING TRASH AND PLASTIC INTO THE OCEAN IS ONE TYPE OF POLLUTION.

HABITATS

A habitat is where an animal or plant lives. Some animals live in deserts, and others in forests. Some live in the seas, and others live in the trees!

THESE BEARS ALL LIVE IN THE FOREST.

It is important to protect animals and their habitats to keep our planet healthy. We must make sure that no habitats are destroyed by humans.

OH NO! THIS BABY RACOON HAS LOST HER HABITAT BECAUSE PEOPLE CUT DOWN ALL THE TREES IN HER HOME.

EXTINCTION

Animals can become extinct if their habitats are destroyed. This means that those animals are no longer alive on Earth.

DINOSAURS BECAME EXTINCT A VERY LONG TIME AGO.

You can help keep habitats safe by looking after the wildlife around you. Try getting your friends together and clean up your favorite park!

KEEPING YOUR PARK GREEN AND CLEAN WILL HELP THE ANIMALS!

BUZZING BEES

Bees are very important for the environment. They are great at <u>pollinating</u> plants, which helps grow new plants. We need bees to grow lots of our food. Sadly, many bees are dying out.

BEES ARE DISAPPEARING BECAUSE THEIR HABITATS ARE BEING DESTROYED BY POLLUTION AND <u>CLIMATE CHANGE</u>.

Did you know that you can take small steps to help our little buzzing friends? Try planting lots of new flowers in your garden for the bees to get their food from!

15

SAVE THE ALBATROSSES!

Albatrosses are found flying over many oceans. Sadly, many are in danger because of all the plastic pollution in the sea. Albatrosses might swallow or get caught in plastic.

ALBATROSS

MORE THAN NINE OUT OF TEN ALBATROSSES HAVE PLASTIC INSIDE OF THEM.

16

IT IS IMPORTANT TO RECYCLE.

You can help save albatrosses by using less plastic and recycling it properly. Try to reuse as much plastic as possible too.

SAVE THE ORANGUTANS!

Orangutans live in the rain forests of Borneo and Sumatra. Humans are cutting down huge areas of rain forests to make room for farms and buildings. When the orangutans' habitat is destroyed, they have nowhere to live.

ORANGUTANS MIGHT BECOME EXTINCT.

Orangutans are <u>endangered</u> animals. You can help save the orangutans by raising money for a charity that protects them.

HAVE A BAKE SALE AND GIVE ALL THE MONEY TO AN ORANGUTAN CHARITY!

Bake Sale

Today

XIYE BASTIDA

This is Xiye Bastida. She is an <u>activist</u> who is helping the environment by speaking about how dangerous pollution is. Xiye wants everyone to make less pollution and work together to help save Earth.

XIYE BASTIDA

Xiye wants to protect animals from pollution. She is trying to get people to listen to her and find ways to look after our planet.

WILL YOU HELP XIYE SAVE THE PLANET?

MAKE YOUR OWN RECYCLED BIRD FEEDER

Here is what you need to make a recycled bird feeder.

TWO PENCILS

SOME STRING

SCISSORS

BIRD FOOD

PLASTIC BOTTLE

STEP 1: Ask an adult to cut a hole in the side of the bottle big enough for a bird to feed from.

STEP 2: Poke a few small holes in the bottom so rainwater can get out.

STEP 3: Stick the pencils through the bottle near the hole for birds to stand on.

STEP 4: Fill the bottle with bird food. Tie a string around the bottle neck and hang it outside.

GLOSSARY

activist	someone who tries to make a change by speaking out
climate change	a change in the typical weather or temperature of a large area
endangered	when a species of animal is in danger of going extinct
environment	the natural world
landscape	a part of a natural area such as a river, field, or mountain
pollinating	passing on pollen from a plant to another plant of the same kind, so that seeds will be produced
pollution	something added to our environment that is harmful to living things
recycle	use again to make something else
species	a group of very similar animals or plants that can create young together

INDEX